Curse Words Coloring Book for Adults

Randy Johnson

ISBN: 9781520548753
ISBN-13: 9781520548753

DEDICATION

"Here's to the angry ones."

Bullshit

Shit

Fuck

Piss Off

Bitch

Damn

Shitballs

Bollocks

Crap

Fucktard

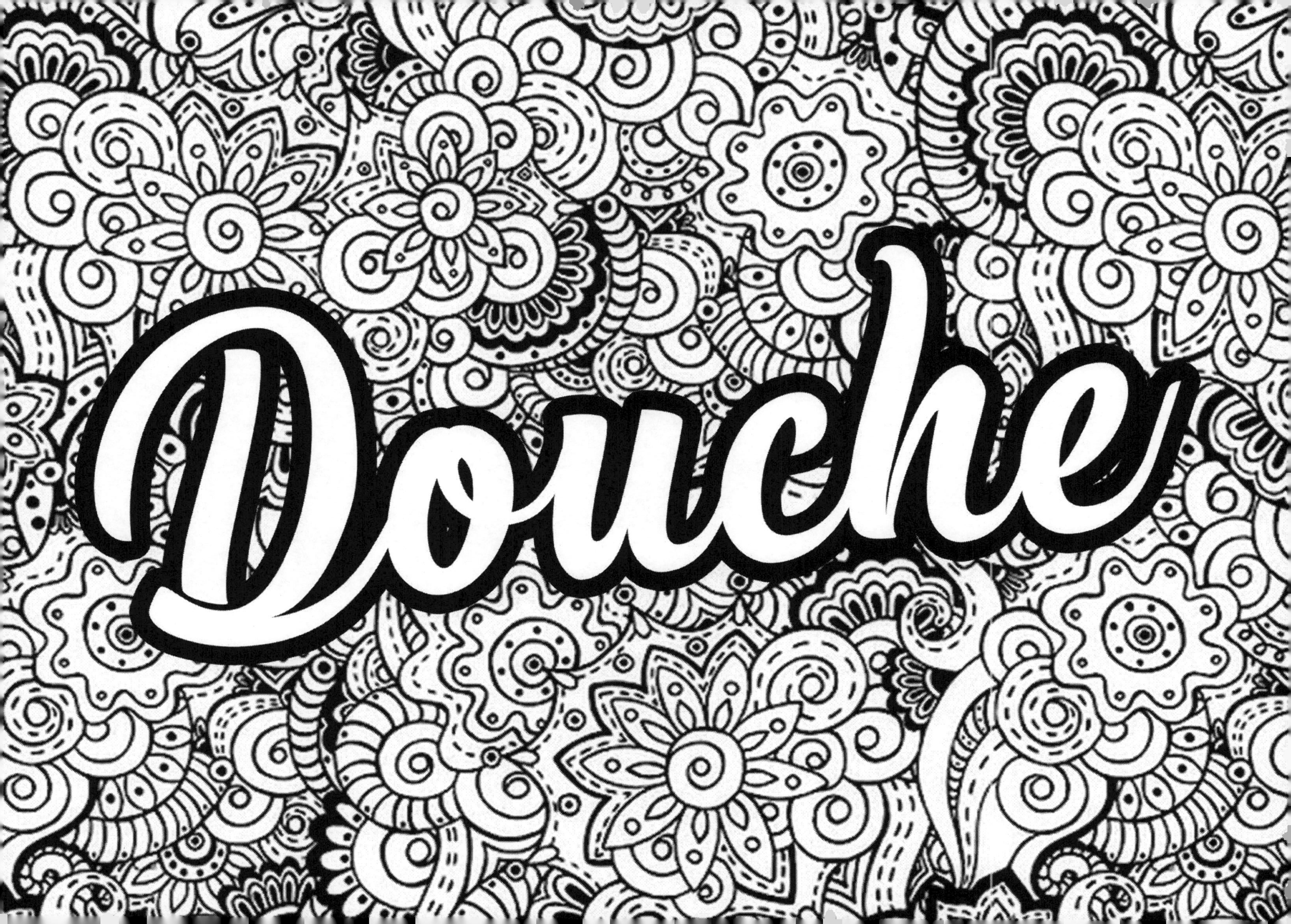
Douche

Chode

Asshole

Whore

Wanker

Slut

Fuckballs

Cunt

Asshat

Bastard

Sugartits

skank

Fuck Boy

Twat
Waffle

Dipshit

Shit-a-brick

piss flaps

Moron

Baggy
Vag

Fuck Off

Cum
Guzzler

Idiot

Dickhead

Slutbag

Cockbag

Beaver
Dam

Shitbag
COFFEE

prick

Cunt
Cake

Fuck
Nugget

Piece of Shit

Twat

Cum Dumpster

Thunder
Cunt

Jizz
Mopper

Fucker

Flip-a-Bitch

Asswipes

Tramp

Crack-whore

85656021R00060

Made in the USA
San Bernardino, CA
21 August 2018